KENT BUSES

JOHN LAW

AMBERLEY

A typical scene in Maidstone High Street as Maidstone & District 5906 (K906 SKR) loads up in March 1993. This Northern Counties-bodied Leyland Olympian had been bought new only a few weeks earlier.

First published 2019

Amberley Publishing
The Hill, Stroud
Gloucestershire, GL5 4EP

www.amberley-books.com

Copyright © John Law, 2019

The right of John Law to be identified as the Author of this work has been asserted in accordance with the Copyrights, Designs and Patents Act 1988.

ISBN 978 1 4456 8896 1 (print)
ISBN 978 1 4456 8897 8 (ebook)

All rights reserved. No part of this book may be reprinted or reproduced or utilised in any form or by any electronic, mechanical or other means, now known or hereafter invented, including photocopying and recording, or in any information storage or retrieval system, without the permission in writing from the Publishers.

British Library Cataloguing in Publication Data.
A catalogue record for this book is available from the British Library.

Origination by Amberley Publishing.
Printed in the UK.

Introduction

Kent is a county of real contrasts. There are commuter towns for London, hop fields for the beer industry, and plenty of orchards; indeed it is known as the 'Garden of England'. Despite some beautiful natural scenery, there is still a lot of industry, especially in North Kent and the Lower Medway Valley. Chalk quarrying and paper making, though much declined, have left their mark over the landscape.

In East Kent, coal mining was a major employer until the 1980s. The coastal communities provide holiday resorts for Londoners while also hosting the main ports for the near continent.

The county boundaries were unchanged until 1965, when towns like Bexley and Bromley were transferred to Greater London. Surprisingly, Dartford remained in Kent.

Like other counties, public transport started with farmers' carts being adapted to take people into market towns to buy or sell produce. The first tramway in Kent came in 1891 when the Folkestone, Hythe & Sandgate Tramway was opened. Operated by horse-drawn cars, it never actually reached Folkestone and closure came in 1921.

The port of Dover was the first in Kent to have an electric tramway system, opening in 1897. Twenty years later, the town was to see Britain's worst tram disaster when eleven passengers were killed after a tram ran away down Crabble Hill. Dover's tram system closed in 1936.

The early years of the twentieth century saw more Kentish locations gain tramways, with the Thanet towns' system opening in 1901, followed by Gravesend and Chatham in 1902. During the following year the tiny route in Sheerness-on-Sea began operations, followed by a more substantial network in the county town of Maidstone in 1904. Sheerness only lasted until 1917, whereas the trams in Maidstone eventually succumbed to trolleybuses in 1930.

Trolleybuses also eventually replaced part of the final Kent tram system to open, operated by Dartford Council from 1906. In 1933 that town's trams were taken over by London Transport, who replaced them with trolleybuses in 1935 as far as the town centre on route 696.

London Transport's interest in West Kent began in 1933 when the organisation was founded and extended well beyond the boundaries of the metropolis. The green 'country' buses reached Gravesend and Sevenoaks, with a Green Line route running all the way to Tunbridge Wells.

On the first day of 1970 London Country Bus Services became a new National Bus Company subsidiary, formed to take over the former country services of London Transport. An ageing fleet of AEC buses was inherited but was eventually modernised with Leyland Atlanteans, Leyland Nationals and comfortable coaches.

In preparation for privatisation, London Country was split into four businesses, with London Country South East taking over most of the Kentish operations. This soon changed its name to become Kentish Bus, with its headquarters at Northfleet Garage. The company became part of Proudmutual in 1988, joining forces with Northumbria Motor Services.

The British Bus Group purchased Proudmutual in 1994, becoming the Cowie Group in 1997, who quickly brought the brand name Arriva to all its operations. Arriva itself is now part of Deutsche Bahn.

The main bus operator in the central area of Kent, including Tonbridge, Maidstone and the Medway towns, was Maidstone & District Motor Services, which was registered as a limited company in 1911. It was acquired by British Electric Traction in 1913 and rapidly expanded. An interesting development was the opening of the country's first bus station in 1922.

Maidstone & District (M&DMS) became part of the National Bus Company in 1969, adopting the standard leaf green livery. By then a fleet of mainly, but not exclusively, Leyland vehicles was owned. Privatisation occurred in 1986, in the form of a management buy-out. This lasted until 1995, when British Bus took over. M&DMS then followed the same path as Kentish Bus and is now part of Arriva.

Right in the heart of M&DMS territory was the only municipal operator to survive the demise of its trams: Maidstone Corporation. After it dispensed with its trolleybuses in 1967, a fleet of Leyland double-deck buses was employed, newly painted in a blue and cream livery. Unusually, lightweight Bedford saloons were purchased to replace the 'deckers, though a batch of ex-Nottingham 'Lilac' Leyland Leopards was also acquired.

In 1986, Maidstone Borough Council Transport, as it had become, was rebranded as Boro'line, with a yellow and blue colour scheme. Deregulation and the tendering process saw operations started beyond the council boundaries, particularly in London. Financial difficulties later occurred, with the London operations being sold to Kentish Bus and the rest of the assets going to M&DMS in 1992.

One other council scheme remains to be mentioned, in that Kent County Council began running its own bus services from 2005 until 2013, under the name of Kent Top Travel.

The area of the county furthest away from the capital soon became the territory of the East Kent Road Car Company. This had been formed in 1916 when various small businesses were amalgamated. Like M&DMS, it became part of British Electric Traction, following the same road into the National Bus Company. By that time, the fleet consisted of mainly AEC vehicles, with the fine maroon livery being replaced by poppy red.

The East Kent Road Car Company was sold to a management buy-out in 1987, which brought back a modernised version of the old colours. Sadly, this was not to last and the Stagecoach Group took over in 1993.

Today the county is dominated by two players: Arriva and Stagecoach. Other operators have been, and in some cases still are, present. Southdown once ran into Tunbridge Wells, with Brighton & Hove taking over. London & Country could occasionally be found in Sevenoaks. Even Eastbourne Buses once ran a service into Kent! Go-Ahead Group-owned Metrobus can also be found in the west of the county.

Since the 1960s the independent sector has not been very strong in Kent. Dengate's Rye operations, which crossed the border into Kent, succumbed to M&DMS in 1974, leaving only a handful of services in the hands of Drew's of Canterbury, Thames-Weald, etc. Donsway gained a toehold in the Faversham area in the 1980s.

This all changed after deregulation in 1986. Various companies gained council-tendered contracts, while other tried competitive services in and around the major conurbations. A lot, including Bygone Buses, Fuggles, and Eastonways, have fallen by the wayside. However, there are still a few independents around, the largest being Nu-Venture.

The county of Kent is still a great place of interest to the present-day bus enthusiast, with plenty of variety and, of course, some lovely countryside and historical sites. This book has attempted to illustrate the public road transport of the county since the 1970s.

Finally, thanks to the late Les Flint and Jim Sambrooks for supplying a few photographs to fill in a couple of gaps in the author's collection. Thanks also to Bus Lists on the Web for providing a one-stop source of information during the research for this book.

Maidstone was once home to a small tram system, which opened in 1904. Shortly after that, one of the four-wheeled cars is seen in the town's High Street, having just arrived from Barming. The trams ceased operating in 1930. (Author's Collection)

Trolleybuses replaced Maidstone's trams on the Barming route in 1928 and two of the original double-deck vehicles, 13 and 14, are seen in the High Street around that time. Maidstone Corporation finally disposed of its trolleybus fleet in 1967, when motor buses took over. The business was renamed Maidstone Borough Council Transport in line with political changes in 1974. (Author's Collection)

By the mid-1970s the Maidstone Borough Council bus fleet consisted mainly of Leyland double-deck vehicles. This older example, seen in the High Street c. 1975, was 10 (410 DKM). The sixty-one-seat Massey-bodied Leyland PD2/30 had been new in 1958.

At the same spot as the top picture, albeit on a sunny day, Maidstone Borough Council 31 (EKP 231C) sits awaiting departure for the suburb of Tovil. The bus is again bodied by Massey, seating seventy-four passengers, on a Leyland Atlantean PDR1/1 chassis.

In the 1970s Maidstone Borough Council turned to lightweight Bedfords for their bus requirements. A batch of Willowbrook-bodied YRQ types was received first, followed by YRT/Duple Dominant saloons delivered in 1975. One example, 53 (JKO 63N), was photographed in the High Street when only a year old.

Maidstone also bought a few Lilac Leopards from Nottingham City Transport. These were Leyland Leopards with Duple Dominant coach-type bodywork, fitted with folding doors and fifty-three bus seats. One of them, 24 (HNU 124N), is seen beside All Saints Church in Maidstone town centre on a cold day in 1978.

Only four Bedford JJL bus chassis were ever produced and all were sold to Maidstone Borough Council. EKX 648T had been new as a demonstrator and is seen at Maidstone's depot in 1981. Like the other three, it had Marshall twenty-four-seat bodywork. The JJL buses did not last long in Kent, with three going to Brighton and one to Bournemouth.

In the early 1980s Maidstone again turned to Bedford for its new buses. Fleet number 182 (MKP 182W) was one of a batch of YMT type chassis fitted with sixty-one-seat bodywork by Wadham Stringer. It is seen in the new brown and cream colour scheme on the High Street in 1981.

Maidstone Borough Council bought six unusual vehicles in 1982, two of which are illustrated here at Borough Green railway station in spring 1983. They are both ready to depart on a rail replacement service to their home town. 142 and 143 (CKN 142/3Y) feature rare (for the time) Wright bodywork on Bedford YMT chassis.

In the years following deregulation, Maidstone Borough Council's fleet was given the title of 'Boro'line' and the livery was changed to yellow and blue. These colours are seen applied to 207 (D207 MKK), a sixty-four-seat Scania K92CRS bodied by East Lancs. Bought new in early 1987, it was photographed in Maidstone High Street towards the end of that year.

In the late 1980s Maidstone Boro'line undertook some tendered work in Greater London, which is why 917 (NSP 319R) is carrying London Transport logos. However, in this photograph, taken in December 1989, it is seen in Maidstone's High Street. This Alexander-bodied Volvo Ailsa B55-10 had been new in 1976 to Tayside Regional Transport in Dundee.

Another double-decker captured on film on Maidstone's High Street in December 1989, fleet number 273 (OTO 559M) had originated with Nottingham City Transport. It is a Leyland Atlantean AN68/1R with East Lancs bodywork to Nottingham's own specification.

The Medway towns were once served by a sizeable tramway network operated by the Chatham & District Light Railways, opening between 1902 and 1908 on both sides of the Medway itself. Seen around 1910 on leafy New Road, Rochester, is four-wheel car 40, built by Brush of Loughborough. In 1927, the system was purchased by bus company Maidstone & District and the final trams ceased operating in 1930. The Chatham & District fleet name and a separate livery were applied to M&D buses in the area until the 1950s. (Author's Collection)

The name 'Maidstone & District Motor Services' (M&DMS) was registered in 1911, though the origins of the company began a few years earlier. By 1914, when this photograph was taken, services had considerably expanded and this Daimler saloon, registered KT.1435, is seen in Maidstone prior to its departure for Hastings. M&DMS later became part of the British Electric Traction (BET) Group. (Author's Collection)

In BET days Maidstone & District utilised a dark green colour scheme, with cream where appropriate. This was reversed on coaches and dual-purpose vehicles. Still wearing that livery, with its traditional-style fleet name, is AEC Reliance/Weymann DP49F 2557 (BKT 820C), photographed in Gravesend in 1974.

As early as 1974, the NBC logo and lettering was being quickly applied to M&DMS vehicles. Painted in the old dark green livery, but now bearing its new identity, is 3694 (194 XKE), a forty-two-seat AEC Reliance/Harrington bus, seen passing J. S. Tidby's wine merchants in Tunbridge Wells.

In the company of a London Country RT trainer bus at Sevenoaks bus station in 1974 is M&DMS 3761 (31 YKK). New in 1963 as SC31, this is another AEC Reliance, bodied by Willowbrook, with forty-nine dual-purpose seats. In this photograph, however, it has been downgraded to bus duties and is seen newly painted in NBC green.

Here is another AEC Reliance, this time bodied by Marshall, with fifty-three bus seats. 3708 (BKT 823C) still has its BET-style colours, having just arrived in Tunbridge Wells, again in 1974.

Maidstone & District's AEC Reliance 392 DKK was new in 1958 as fleet number CO392 and carried a forty-one-seat Harrington coach body. It was later heavily rebuilt as a service bus and is seen as such, numbered 3351 and still in dark green, inside Maidstone depot, around 1974.

Another AEC Reliance/Harrington coach combination, still used on frontline duties in 1974, was 4023 (23 TKR). This well-proportioned 'Cavalier' thirty-seven-seat vehicle was found in the depot yard in Maidstone.

A really unusual coach in the M&DMS fleet was 4703 (7013 HN), a 1962-built Bristol MW6G with fine ECW coachwork. It had been new to United Automobile Services as fleet number BUC13. It was photographed, *c.* 1974, at Maidstone depot.

As well as the AEC Reliances that we have already seen, Maidstone & District also bought large batches of Leyland Leopard saloons, one of which, 3428 (AKM 428K), is seen on Mount Pleasant Road in Tunbridge Wells in 1974. The forty-five-seat Willowbrook body is still painted in the pre-NBC colours.

The business of John Dengate & Son of Rye, Sussex, was taken over by Maidstone & District in 1974. Later in that year, LJH 252L, a forty-nine-seat dual-purpose Leyland Leopard/Willowbrook saloon, was photographed at Northiam in Kent. The vehicle is still in Dengate's livery, but NBC-style names have been applied. It will soon receive fleet number 2852.

Another Maidstone & District AEC Reliance is illustrated here, in Sevenoaks, in 1974. 3710 (BKT 825C) carries fifty-three-seat Marshall bodywork.

Maidstone & District was one of the first companies to order rear-engined Leyland Atlantean double-deck buses. Delivered as DH624 in 1963, it is seen as 5624 (624 UKM), still in pre-NBC colours, out of use at Maidstone depot around 1976. It is of the PDR1/1 type and has seventy-seven-seat Weymann bodywork.

Some of the early Atlanteans had a good long life. An example is 5596 (596 UKM), another 1963-built Weymann-bodied bus. It is seen, still in front-line service, at Luton depot, Chatham, in 1980. Note the large fleet number over the front upper-deck windows. This enabled the inspector at the Pentagon bus station in Chatham to keep an eye on timekeeping from his lofty eyrie.

Here is as view of the M&DMS Luton depot in Chatham. Closest to the camera and still in the old colours in the mid-1970s is 6074 (74 YKT), which was one the earliest of a large batch of seventy-seven-seat Northern Counties-bodied Daimler Fleetlines delivered between 1963 and 1968.

Another Daimler Fleetline/Northern Counties, 6102 (FKL 111D), new in 1966, is seen in central Tunbridge Wells in 1974, newly painted in NBC green.

For further double-deck requirements, Maidstone & District turned back to the Leyland Atlantean during 1972/3. Part of a batch of twenty, 5717 (FKM 717L) is a PDR1A/1 with seventy-eight-seat MCW bodywork. It is seen alongside an earlier Atlantean at Gillingham depot, probably in late 1974.

More Daimler Fleetlines were received in 1970, but, unusually, they were single-deck buses. 3824 (SKO 824H), seen here at Gillingham bus station (alongside the depot), carries a Marshall forty-five-seat body fitted with dual doorways. This type of saloon did not find favour with M&DMS and some had already been disposed of by the time of this photograph, c. 1974.

Unusually, Maidstone & District received a dozen Alexander-bodied Daimler Fleetline double-deck buses from Northern General. 5011 (GCN 813G) had been new as No. 2183 in 1969. It is seen in M&DMS hands on a rail replacement service at Rainham station in 1978.

In 1975 M&DMS was allocated two small batches of rare (for the National Bus Company) double-deck buses as a trial, these being Scania Metropolitans and Volvo Ailsas. Initially based at Hastings, they were later transferred to Luton depot, Chatham. One of the Metropolitans, 5251 (KKO 251P), a seventy-five-seat vehicle, was photographed at its home in the summer of 1980.

One of the aforementioned Volvo Ailsa B55-10/Alexander seventy-nine-seat double-deckers, 5381 (LKP 391P) was captured on film on Gillingham High Street *c.* 1979. Neither of the two types of trial vehicles resulted in further orders, though M&DMS later purchased some MCW Metrobuses.

The mid to late 1970s saw the National Bus Company buying various lightweight single-deck buses and Maidstone & District was no exception. 3266 (MKL 266P) was one such example, a forty-three-seat Ford R1014/Plaxton found inside Maidstone depot in August 1980. (Les Flint)

Maidstone & District 2151 (BKJ 151T) was one of many Duple-bodied Leyland Leopard coaches purchased around the end of the 1970s. Designated as a dual-purpose vehicle, it is seen outside Gillingham depot in spring 1980.

Like most other NBC firms, Maidstone & District took a large number of Bristol VR types. The one illustrated here is an ECW-bodied VRT/SL3/6LX delivered in January 1975. 5102 (KKM 102P) is seen leaving the Pentagon bus station, situated around the shopping centre in Chatham, in 1981. A new bus station at street level has since replaced this facility.

Unusually, during its later NBC days, Maidstone & District took delivery of Dennis Dominator double-deck buses. An example is 5303 (FKM 303V), with a Willowbrook seventy-four-seat body. It is seen in the Pentagon bus station, Chatham, in the summer of 1980, only a few months after being built.

As mentioned earlier, M&DMS also bought a batch of MCW Metrobus vehicles, an example of which was photographed leaving the Pentagon bus station in Chatham in 1981. 5270 (FKM 270V), part of a batch received a year earlier, is a seventy-six-seat bus with MCW bodywork.

As well as the more unusual double-deck buses of the previous page, Maidstone & District gained a sizeable number of Leyland Olympians, such as 5888 (A888 PKR). This seventy-seven-seat ECW-bodied bus had been originally intended for Devon General. It is seen carrying an advert for BBC Radio Kent as it leaves the Pentagon bus station in Chatham in late 1986.

The later part of the 1980s saw M&DMS purchasing a number of second-hand buses. One of them, 5307 (XRF 22S), was found outside Chatham railway station in autumn 1986, heading for the suburb of Borstal, after which the reform school system was named. This Dennis Dominator/East Lancs bus had been new in 1978 as 22 in the fleet of East Staffordshire District Council of Burton-on-Trent.

Another used bus acquired by Maidstone & District was 5729 (SRJ 751R). This Northern Counties-bodied Leyland Atlantean AN68A/1R had been part of a 1977 delivery to Greater Manchester Transport. It was photographed close to Tonbridge railway station in the spring of 1989, by which time M&DMS had become part of British Bus. Note the new style of fleet name.

Some vehicles in the British Bus-owned M&DMS received an updated livery in the late 1990s. 3193 (P193 LKJ) looks smart as it sits in Maidstone's High Street in late 1998. This Dennis Dart SLF/Plaxton B40F had been constructed in 1997. The colour scheme, though attractive, did not last long, as Maidstone & District was absorbed into the Arriva empire a few months before this photograph was taken.

The early history of public transport in East Kent included some of the earliest tram systems in England. The largest in this area was the network of the Isle of Thanet Tramways & Lighting Company, which commenced operations in 1901, serving the adjoining towns of Margate, Broadstairs and Ramsgate. It is in the latter location that we see car 2, one of the original St Louis Car Co. trams, climbing away from the harbour. The Thanet tram system closed in 1937, when East Kent Road Car Co. took over the services. (Author's Collection)

Until the days of the National Bus Company, the East Kent Road Car Company employed a fine maroon-based livery as seen on GJG 740D. This AEC Regent V with seventy-two-seat Park Royal bodywork was one of many owned and is seen in Folkestone bus station in June 1974. Note that, at the time of this photograph, East Kent did not use a fleet numbering system, relying on registration marks with unique numbers instead. (Les Flint)

East Kent also had a batch of full-fronted AEC Regent V/Park Royal double-deck buses, which were being withdrawn in the early 1970s. Seen during its last days in 1974 is seventy-two-seat PFN 865, on loan to neighbours Maidstone & District at Luton depot, Chatham.

A few of the full-front AEC Regent V buses had an extended life by virtue of being converted to open-top. One example was PFN 870, built in 1959 and seen by Margate harbour on 4 August 1980. By then it had been given fleet number 7870. Note the unusual version of NBC livery. (Les Flint)

In the 1960s East Kent purchased a small batch of Marshall-bodied Bedford VAS1 buses, a type of vehicle mainly ordered by local councils for non-PSV duties. Around 1975, KJG 112E, a twenty-nine-seater, was photographed in the yard of Ashford depot. Some of this batch survived just long enough to receive NBC red livery.

East Kent certainly liked their AEC Reliances! One of many similar vehicles, TFN 406 was bought new as a forty-one-seat dual-purpose Park Royal-bodied saloon in 1960. It is seen, alongside newer VJG 198J, bodied by Marshall, on a sunny day at Ashford depot c. 1975.

Looking magnificent just inside the depot at Dover in its old livery sometime around 1974/5 is AFN 493B. This is a thirty-four-seat Duple Commander coach body on, of course, an AEC Reliance chassis.

East Kent did not like parting with their beloved AEC Reliances. 521 FN was originally a Park Royal-bodied coach built in 1962. Ten years later it was given a new forty-nine-seat Plaxton Elite body, as seen inside Ashford depot in 1974.

East Kent's later AEC Regent V double-deck buses survived long enough to receive NBC red paintwork. This is seen applied to WFN 839, built in 1961 as a standard Park Royal-bodied vehicle with seventy-two seats. It is seen resting among its fellow AEC types in the yard of Herne Bay depot, c. 1977.

One of the 1966 batch of AEC Regent V/Park Royal buses of East Kent received an all-over advert livery for early colour TV by Rediffusion. GJG 751D is seen at the top end of Wellesley Road in Ashford in 1974. Not long after the photograph was taken, the Duke of Marlborough pub, seen in the background, was demolished.

Weekend engineering works on British Rail's Southern Region could often produce dismay when a rail replacement service was announced. All could be forgiven when one realised that the few miles from Rainham to Sittingbourne would be undertaken aboard East Kent 1963-built AEC Regent V 6789 FN. The year of this photograph was around 1975.

More AEC buses are visible in this view of Canterbury bus station in 1974, all still in the old colours. Closest to the camera is AEC Reliance/Marshall fifty-one-seat saloon KJG 580E, while similar OFN 718F and AEC Regent V 6789 FN are also included.

Unusually, over twenty Leyland Leopard saloons were obtained from Southdown Motor Services in 1971. One of them was 289 AUF with Marshall B49F bodywork, which is seen in Folkestone's bus station in 1974.

For a short while, East Kent also acquired a few ex-Maidstone & District Leyland Atlantean PDR1/1 double-deckers bodied by Metro-Cammell. 572 RKJ is seen in Ashford, *c.* 1976, in NBC red on route 10 (Folkestone to Maidstone), a joint service with M&DMS.

East Kent had a small fleet of service vehicles, including a Guy Arab IV/Park Royal registered GFN 928, which had been cut down to open-top for tree-lopping purposes. In 1980 it is seen in the parking area near Dover's Western Docks alongside GFN 558N, an AEC Reliance/Duple Dominant coach.

One of East Kent's 1967 batch of AEC Regent V double-deckers was also cut down to assist in the removal of tree branches. MFN 939F was photographed resting in the yard of Herne Bay depot in autumn 1984.

East Kent retained Leyland Tiger TS8/Park Royal coach JG 9938 as a heritage vehicle that also acted as a mobile booking office. Sometime in the mid to late 1970s it was photographed outside of its home territory, at Sheerness-on-Sea. This fine old lady still survives in preservation.

By 1980, when fleet numbers had come into use with East Kent, 8526 (526 FN) was found in the yard at Dover Western Docks. This was another of those rebodied AEC Reliances, the chassis being new in 1962, ten years before it gained the Plaxton Elite forty-nine-seat coachwork seen here.

An unusual vehicle to receive National white coach livery was OJG 135F, one of eight listed in the 1974 East Kent fleet list. Despite the bus style of its Willowbrook bodywork, it was fitted with forty-nine coach seats, all on an AEC Reliance chassis. It was found in the parking area of Dover's bus station in 1977.

Here is one of East Kent's twenty-five AEC Reliance/Marshall saloons, each seating fifty-one passengers. Not yet allocated a visible fleet number, VJG 187J was captured on film speeding towards Dover depot for a well-earned break in 1981.

The year 1969 saw East Kent receive its batch of twenty Daimler Fleetlines with seventy-two-seat Park Royal bodywork. One of them, RFN 953G, is seen in its original colours on Newington Road, St Lawrence, in Ramsgate, *c.* 1975.

Again it is 1981 and East Kent OFN 715F has not gained a fleet number. It was one of many AEC Reliances to be found in Canterbury bus station on that day. Like the other twenty-five in the batch, it has Marshall B53F bodywork.

East Kent 8030 (HFN 30L), one of ten AEC Reliance/Duple Dominant fifty-one-seat coaches purchased in 1973, is photographed in Folkestone bus station in 1981. The scene has changed little today.

In 1971 East Kent bought a batch of a dozen AEC Swifts with Alexander fifty-one-seat bodies. One of them, YJG 590K, is seen outside Dover Marine railway station on a local service in 1977. Unlike the AEC Reliance, the Swift did not find favour with East Kent and no more were ordered.

For local services in Ashford, East Kent purchased four little Bristol LHS6L/ECW B35F saloons in 1975. Seen when almost new is GFN 559N, photographed on Wellesley Road in Ashford. This type of bus was ideal for negotiating the twisty narrow roads and low railway bridges in the town's suburbs.

Deal depot in 1981 is the location of this photograph of East Kent 8804 (PVB 804S), a 1978-built Leyland Leopard (the AEC Reliance was nearing the end of its production run) with Duple Dominant forty-nine-seat coachwork fitted with folding doors and thus attracting a government grant. Appropriately, it is painted in dual-purpose livery.

Like most NBC subsidiaries, East Kent began to take in Leyland Nationals in the 1970s. One built in 1976, JJG 890P, a fifty-two-seat service bus, is seen at Dover Marine station in 1977.

The year 1976 also saw East Kent buy a small batch of Ford R1014/Plaxton forty-three-seat buses. Allocated fleet number 1331, KFN 331P was photographed at Deal depot in 1981.

For duties within the two main Channel Ports, Dover and Folkestone, East Kent painted buses in various versions of Sealink livery and used them from Dover Priory and Folkestone Central railway stations to connect with the ferries to the Continent. In an early Sealink colour scheme in 1977 we see AEC Regent V/Park Royal GJG 760D passing along Snargate Street in Dover, heading for the Western Docks (not Calais!).

On page 19 of this book is Maidstone & District's SKO 824H. The same vehicle, a Marshall-bodied Daimler Fleetline saloon, was later transferred to East Kent and is seen as fleet number 1824 (not carried at the time) at the Western Docks parking area in Dover in 1980.

The latest Sealink livery at the time is seen applied to East Kent 1560 (GFN 560N), one of the Bristol LHS6L/ECW bought for Ashford local services, in 1981. The location is Folkestone Harbour railway station and 1560 would be used on the shuttle up the hill to Folkestone Central, connecting with stopping services towards London Charing Cross. Folkestone Harbour station and ferry terminal has since closed.

Very much standard NBC double-deck buses, East Kent 7665 and 7665 (XJJ 664/5V) were photographed in Folkestone bus station in 1981. Both are ECW-bodied seventy-four-seat Bristol VRT/SL3/6LXB types.

A sizeable batch of Bristol VRT/SL3/6LXB double-deck buses with Willowbrook H43/31F bodies was ordered for Maidstone & District, but were delivered to East Kent in 1977 and 1978. One of them, 7982 (TFN 982T), is seen in Hythe in 1981. After sale by East Kent, this vehicle was cut down to open-top and used on London sightseeing duties, but was later exported to the United States.

In preparation for privatisation, East Kent was allowed to develop its own livery, as seen applied to 1119 (MFN 119R), a forty-nine-seat Leyland National. It was photographed as darkness approached Canterbury bus station in November 1986.

On the same occasion as the previous photograph we see East Kent 7412 (OTY 412M) in its new colours. This Park Royal-bodied Leyland Atlantean AN68/1R had been new as 179M with Northern General. Originally it had a dual-doorway layout, but had been converted to single-door prior to its journey south.

On 5 March 1987 East Kent Road Car was privatised as the result of a management buyout. The previous livery continued to be applied and is seen on 7844 (HNB 44N) in Canterbury in early 1988. This Leyland Atlantean AN68/1R with Northern Counties bodywork had been originally delivered to Greater Manchester PTE as 7554.

One of the first buses ordered by the privatised East Kent Road Car Company was 7755 (E755 UKR), one of ten MCW Mark II Metrobus double-deckers. It is seen in Snargate Street, Dover, in mid-1988. It later received traditional East Kent livery to celebrate seventy-five years of the business.

Like many other companies, East Kent turned to the minibus to meet some of its needs. Photographed in Dover in March 1993 was 47 (G447 VKK), an Iveco/Fiat 49.10 with twenty-three-seat Carlyle bodywork. An earlier Ford Transit is further down the street.

Another minibus photographed in March 1993, East Kent 116 (J116 LKO) is a further Iveco/Fiat 49.10, this time with Dormobile B23F bodywork. It is seen in Canterbury bus station on a city service.

An unusual vehicle in the East Kent fleet was 8843 (6540 FN), seen in Canterbury in 1990. This MCW Metroliner fifty-one-seat luxury coach had been new to the company in 1983, registered FKK 843Y.

A later version of the MCW Metroliner had much more pleasing lines. East Kent 8246 (XYK 976) had been new to Premier Travel, Cambridge, registered B192 JVA. It was photographed within Dover depot in March 1993. Later that year East Kent was purchased by the Stagecoach Group.

One other former BET company ran into Kent, Southdown Motor Services, on a joint route (with Maidstone & District) from Brighton to Tunbridge Wells. Seen at the latter location in 1974 is 132 (BUF 132C), a Marshall-bodied Leyland Leopard forty-five seat saloon, still in its old light green livery, albeit with NBC identity. The tiny Green Line coach station has long since vanished.

On the first day of 1970 London Transport transferred its 'Country' fleet to the National Bus Company's London Country Bus Services Ltd (LCBS). This included a rather ancient collection of vehicles, an example being this 1951-built AEC Regal IV/Metro-Cammell thirty-nine-seat Green Line 'coach'. RF28 (LYF 379) was photographed, still in Green Line livery, after a long journey from Windsor via Central London, at Tunbridge Wells in 1974. This vehicle has since been preserved.

By 1974 LCBS had begun to modernise the fleet. One of the first NBC standard new buses bought was BL1 (RPH 101L), delivered in October 1973. This Bristol LHS6L with thirty-five-seat ECW bodywork was photographed at Sevenoaks bus station.

London Country's RF types continued to soldier on and, in 1976, RF239 (MLL 776) was found outside Dartford Garage. It is still in the green livery, with yellow trim, that was applied in 1970 or thereabouts. Note the Maidstone Leyland PD2 inside the building (all will be explained on page 54).

LCBS also inherited a large amount of AEC Routemasters from London Transport. Included was RMC1471 (471 CLT), seen in NBC green outside Swanley Garage in 1979. This Park Royal-bodied bus had previously been used on Green Line express duties, hence the platform doors. By the time of this photograph, it had been relegated to local services.

In its early years London Country continued to receive new AEC Swifts that had been ordered by London Transport. New in 1970 was SM114 (BPH 114H), a thirty-eight-seat, dual-doorway, Park Royal saloon, photographed in NBC green at Dartford in 1976.

The year 1971 saw the delivery of SMS493 (DPD 493J) to London Country, this time with forty-one seats inside bodywork by MCW. Again, a dual-doorway layout had been specified. It is seen still in its original livery at Sevenoaks bus station in 1974.

London Country's Green Line services were revolutionised when more modern vehicles arrived. A large batch of Park Royal-bodied AEC Reliances was received, each having forty-five dual-purpose seats. The example here, RP69 (JPA 169K), based at Dunton Green Garage near Sevenoaks, is being used on a normal bus route when photographed at Riverhill in June 1975. (Les Flint)

Another London Country garage in Kent, at Northfleet near Gravesend, was allocated a small number of AEC Swifts with Alexander DP45F bodies. The example here, SMA10 (JPF 110K), was photographed sitting in the sun at its home depot c. 1977.

Swanley Garage began to receive dual-purpose Leyland Nationals for Green Line duties in the mid-1970s, the examples here being SNC170 (HPF 320N) and SNC197 (LPB 197P), both seating thirty-nine passengers on comfortable seats. They are photographed in the yard at Swanley sometime around 1978.

Most LCBS garages received a goodly number of Leyland Atlantean PDR1A/1 Special AN class double-deckers and Dunton Green was no exception. Photographed outside its home on 17 October 1982 was AN24, which had Park Royal H43/29D bodywork. It had been transferred here only a year earlier. This bus later passed to Kentish Bus and eventually ended up with North Western Road Car until it was scrapped in 1991. (Les Flint)

LCBS BN54 (TPJ 54S) was new to Dunton Green Garage, near Sevenoaks, in 1977 and is seen posing at its home not long after delivery. Looking very smart in NBC green, it is a Bristol LHS6L with ECW thirty-five-seat bodywork.

This 'B' type (built without the familiar roof-mounted heating pod) Leyland National forty-one-seat bus, SNB486 (BPL 486T), was delivered to LCBS in 1979 and was found in the yard of Dartford Garage in 1980.

Delivery of 'proper' coaches for London Country's Green Line services began in 1977 and continued into the early 1980s, with a large fleet of AEC Reliances being purchased, initially bodied by Plaxton and later by Duple. One of the latter, RB133 (EPM 133V), was photographed at Dunton Green Garage during 1980 in special colours celebrating the golden jubilee of Green Line services. (Les Flint)

The aging stock inherited from London Transport by LCBS meant that vehicle shortages were suffered during the mid-1970s. In 1975 Western National's Royal Blue 1406 (744 MDV) was on loan and was photographed by the late Les Flint (a Dunton Green driver at the time) at Chevening in 1975.

Maidstone Borough Transport 12 (412 DKM) was on loan to London Country in 1976. This Massey-bodied Leyland PD2/30, seating sixty-one passengers, is seen arriving at Dartford Garage.

LCBS also hired buses from Eastbourne Borough Transport, including 65 (JJK 265), a 1965-built AEC Regent V with East Lancs bodywork. This fine vehicle is seen heading out from Dartford town centre on the 477 route to Chelsfield, *c.* 1975

In 1986 LCBS was split up in preparation for privatisation. Services in Kent came under the umbrella of London Country South East, soon rebranded as Kentish Bus. A smart new livery was introduced and is seen applied to 662 (EPH 205V). This was previously AN205 in the LCBS fleet. This 1979-built Leyland Atlantean AN68A/1R with Roe bodywork is seen in Sevenoaks bus station in April 1990.

Kentish Bus was not immune to the fashion for minibus operation in the years after deregulation. Several Talbot Pullman three-axle vehicles with Talbot bodies were obtained, seating twenty-two people. One, 872 (G872 SKE), was photographed in April 1990 passing Sevenoaks railway station, about a mile (all uphill!) from the town centre.

In 1998 Kentish Bus had been sold to a management buyout team called Proudmutual Ltd, who also owned Northumbria Motor Services. A transfer from that operation was Kentish Bus 302 (WDC 220Y), an ECW-bodied Leyland Olympia. It is seen in Dartford in spring 1991. Four years later it passed to Arriva Cymru.

B series Leyland National 465 (YPL 439T) was found parked in Sevenoaks bus station in autumn 1987. It had been new as a short forty-one-seat saloon with London Country as SNB439 in 1978. In 1992 East Lancs Coachbuilders rebuilt it to 'Greenway' standard.

Another minibus in the Kentish Bus fleet was 868 (E675 DCU), a MCW Metrorider that had come from Northumbria, but had been new to Moor-Dale Coaches in 1987. It was found beside Gravesend railway station in March 1993.

In the spring of 1991 Kentish Bus was operating Green Line service 726 with coach 228 (SND 296X), photographed in Dartford. This Plaxton-bodied Leyland Leopard had been new to National Travel (West) in 1981. At the time of this photograph the 726 service ran from Dartford to Heathrow Airport, but has since been cut back, starting its westbound journey at Croydon, and has also been rebadged as X26.

A more modern coach was found at the Kentish Bus garage in Northfleet on a wet day in March 1993: 27 (OSK 776), in a special 'Kentish Express' livery. It had been new to LCBS as a Green Line Leyland Tiger/Berkhof fifty-three-seat vehicle, registered C150 SPB.

In 1994 the Proudmutual Group, including Kentish Bus, became part of British Bus and a new green and yellow livery was introduced. It is seen applied to 231 (EPH 231V), a former London Country Leyland Atlantean AN68A/1R with Roe bodywork, originally numbered AN231. It is seen in Tunbridge Wells in early 1997, less than a year after the Cowie Group had acquired British Bus.

Kentish Bus 259 (N259 BKK), a Scania L113CRL with low-floor forty-three-seat Wright bodywork, had been delivered to Kentish Bus in December 1995. Only a few months later it was photographed on service outside Dartford Library, a building dating back to 1916. In 1997 the Cowie Group was rebranded as Arriva and that company's vehicles are shown on page 62 and beyond.

When LCBS was split, the Surrey area operations became London Country South West, later known as London & Country. This company, like Kentish Bus, became part of British Bus, but retained a separate identity for many years. Its main bus service into Kent was the 410 route, terminating a Sevenoaks, where AD9 (N809 TPK) is seen in the new bus station in early 1997. It is a rare Dennis Arrow with East Lancs bodywork to coach specification. Like Kentish Bus, London & Country was soon absorbed into Arriva.

Part of the Go-Ahead Group, Brighton & Hove run regular services from East Sussex into Tunbridge Wells. Here, on 18 May 2007, we see 777 (P877 VFG). This East Lancs-bodied Scania N113DRB had been new to the company in 1997.

Metrobus also became part of the Go-Ahead Group in 1999. Today the company operates throughout East Sussex, Surrey and into parts of Kent. Again, Tunbridge Wells, on 18 May 2007, is the location and 376 (Y376 HMY) is the subject of the photograph. This Dennis Dart SLF with Caetano thirty-eight-seat bodywork had been new to Metrobus in 2001.

Another Metrobus vehicle, 471 (YN53 USG), was found in Tunbridge Wells on 7 July 2009, coming down the hill past the railway station. This Scania N94UD has East Lancs 'Omnidekka' dual-doorway bodywork.

One other large operator to be featured, brought about by deregulation, the tendering process and privatisation, is Eastbourne Buses, a business that expanded beyond its traditional municipal boundaries. Fleet number 54 (GX02 WXW), a thirty-four-seat DAF/Wright saloon, was photographed in Tunbridge Wells *c*. 2005. Eastbourne Buses was later taken over by Stagecoach.

In 1997 the former British Bus/Cowie operations were all rebranded under the name of Arriva, reuniting all the ex-London Country subsidiaries, plus Maidstone & District. A new blue-based livery was soon introduced as seen on 5917 (M917 MKM). This Volvo Olympian with seventy-seven-seat Northern Counties bodywork had been inherited from Maidstone & District. Photographed on 27 August 2007, the vehicle is parked in the combined bus station and depot at Hawkhurst, which has since closed.

Found on 18 May 2007 on Maidstone's High Street was Arriva 5563 (L563 YCU). Despite being firmly in former M&DMS territory, this Volvo Olympian/Northern Counties double-deck bus had been new to Kentish Bus.

Arriva 3049 (H256 YLG) had an interesting history. It had started out as a forty-nine-seat Leyland Lynx with Welsh independent Wright's of Wrexham in 1990. The year 1993 saw that company cease operation and the bus passed to a firm in Bootle, Merseyside. Quite how it got into the Arriva fleet remains a mystery, but it is seen here in Maidstone High Street on 18 May 2007.

Number 3022 (N322 TPK) in the Arriva Southern Counties fleet had been new as LS22 with London & Country. This East Lancs-bodied Dennis Lance forty-nine-seat saloon was photographed in Tunbridge Wells town centre on 18 May 2007.

Again on 18 May 2007 we are in Maidstone High Street to witness the arrival of Arriva 3968 (GN04 UGF) in a special 'Park & Ride' livery. This thirty-nine-seat VDL DE02/Wright saloon had been new to Arriva in 2004.

Arriva's London operations today extend into Kent, reaching the Bluewater Shopping Centre. This is where red-liveried ENX27 (GN09 AWF) is heading as it calls at its main stop in Dartford on 6 April 2018. This thirty-two-seat Alexander Dennis Enviro200 with a dual-doorway layout was based at Dartford at the time, despite the red livery.

Arriva's 'Fastrack' services connect Dartford and Gravesend with Bluewater and Ebbsfleet International railway station. They take advantage of priority at traffic lights, bus lanes and short sections of dedicated busways. In the special livery is 4321 (GN15 CXU), a Wright Streetlite DF thirty-seven-seat bus. It is seen in Gravesend on 21 July 2017.

The Wright Streetlite has also found favour in Tunbridge Wells, but as the shorter WF (Wheel Forward) version. 1657 (GN64 DXU), a thirty-seat bus, was photographed as it crossed over the railway in the centre of town on 30 August 2018.

A recent development, welcomed by most, has been the closure of Chatham's Pentagon bus station, being replaced by a new facility at street level. Seen here on 7 February 2018 is Alexander Dennis Enviro E20D 4108 (SN17 MXG) in the latest Arriva livery, which is rapidly being applied throughout the nation.

Volvo 7900E all-electric bus LF67 EVV was loaned to Arriva on a seven-week trial over 'Fastrack' routes. A charging point was installed outside Greenhithe station (the railhead for Bluewater) where the vehicle is getting its five-minute or so burst of 'magic juice' on 6 April 2018. This vehicle, including the land-based equipment, later moved to Cardiff.

East Kent Road Car Company was sold to Stagecoach in 1993 and the famous stripes soon began to appear. In the summer of that year they had been applied to 7750 (E750 SKR), a 1988-built, seventy-seven-seat MCW Metrobus Mark II, seen in the village of Garlinge, on the main road into Margate from the west.

Another ex-East Kent double-deck bus to receive Stagecoach livery, 7809 (H809 BKK) was photographed in December 1998. This Northern Counties-bodied Leyland Olympian is seen in Deal's miniscule bus station, loading up for Canterbury.

Only a few days after the Stagecoach takeover in 1993, 1401 (J401 LKO), which had been delivered to East Kent two years earlier, is seen in Canterbury in 'Park & Ride' livery. It is a DAF SB220 with forty-nine-seat Optare Delta bodywork.

The year 1994 saw more 'Park & Ride' buses delivered to Stagecoach East Kent, including 1408 (M408 OKM), an unusual Berkhof-bodied Dennis Lance SLF. This forty-seat bus is seen passing Canterbury bus station in the summer of 1995.

New to Stagecoach East Kent (internally part of South Coast Buses, hence the Sussex registration), 676 (R676 HCD) was a Plaxton-bodied Volvo B10M-55, seating forty-eight passengers. It is seen in the coastal town of Deal in December 1998.

The twenty-first century saw Stagecoach get rid of its stripes, replacing them with this striking colour scheme. It is seen applied to 20639 (M639 BCD), a Volvo B10M-55 with Alexander PS-type bodywork with forty-eight dual-purpose seats, which is passing Ramsgate's busy harbour on 4 May 2007.

Also seen on 4 May 2007 at Ramsgate Harbour is Stagecoach 34649 (GX54 DWZ). By then the company had introduced a five-figure national numbering scheme. The vehicle is a thirty-eight-seat Dennis Dart SLD bodied by Plaxton. It is operating 'The Loop', which is a high-frequency service serving all the major destinations in Thanet.

The year 2006 saw Stagecoach East Kent take delivery of a batch of the earlier type of Alexander Dennis Enviro300 saloons. One of these forty-eight-seat vehicles, 27518 (GX06 DYY), has just passed under the city wall in Canterbury as it approaches the bus station on 4 February 2010.

Stagecoach has kept its East Kent operations up to date and has taken delivery of many new vehicles. Included in the batch received in 2016 was 15276 (YN16 WVS), a Scania N250UD with the latest style of Alexander Dennis bodywork, capable of seating seventy-one passengers. It is seen in St Peter's Place, Canterbury, on 22 March 2018.

In 2017 Stagecoach introduced the 'Little & Often' services in Ashford, using Mercedes City 45 minibuses seating just seventeen passengers. One of them, 44021 (BV66 GUG), was photographed arriving at Ashford International railway station on 11 April 2017. 'Often' proved popular but 'Little' did not and the minibuses have since been transferred away, to be replaced by Optare Solos.

Kent Top Travel was unusual in that it was owned by Kent County Council. Operations commenced in 2005, competing for tendered routes throughout the county. In Tonbridge High Street on 2 September 2009 we see KX07 HFA, an Alexander Dennis Enviro200 capable of seating thirty-seven passengers.

As well as rural services, Kent Top Travel also ran the 'Park & Ride' services in Canterbury. Some double-deck buses were employed on these duties, but PO58 KRD, an Optare-bodied Volvo B7BLE saloon, has been chosen to illustrate these operations. This forty-three-seat vehicle is seen alongside Fenwick's store in central Canterbury on 4 February 2010. Kent Top Travel ceased trading in 2013.

London operator Grey-Green ventured into Kent in the early 1990s, running services around Tunbridge Wells. 801 (D101 NDW) was a regular performer on such duties. This ex-Merthyr Tydfil Leyland Lynx was photographed in central Tunbridge Wells in early 1993.

Another independent of the early 1990s was East Surrey, who, despite the name, ran into Kent and Sussex. Not far from the boundary is the small Kentish town of Edenbridge, where 30 (H744 LHN) was photographed in spring 1994. This twenty-one-seat CVE Omni, dedicated to the Kent Karrier services, had been new to the company in 1990.

Smith's of Sittingbourne operated stage carriage services around the Swale area in the 1990s. In March 1993 Leyland National ODL 885R is seen outside Sittingbourne railway station. This forty-four-seat vehicle had been new as 885 with Southern Vectis on the Isle of Wight.

One of the most notable independents to operate in Kent was Thames Weald Ltd, with Dr H. N. Hefferman in charge. In an effort to replace rural services abandoned by London Transport, the good doctor began operations (not the medical type!) in the 1960s. A variety of minibuses was owned, including Mercedes OVR 798H, seen near the company's HQ in West Kingsdown in autumn 1978. Over the years Thames Weald reached as far as Maidstone and Southend-on-Sea, but bus services ceased in 1998.

Nu-Venture was founded in the 1960s, operating a fleet of coaches. Today the company concentrates on stage carriage and school contracts. A variety of vehicles have been owned over the years, the majority being second-hand. N2 FPK is no exception. This Dennis Dart/UVG combination had been new to Flightparks of Horley for Gatwick Airport duties. It is seen in the centre of Chatham in the latter half of 2000. The town hall is prominent in the background.

The current livery of Nu-Venture is two-tone green, as seen applied to DS03 SUL. This Caetano-bodied Dennis Dart SLF had, as the registration implies, been new to Hertfordshire operator Sullivan Buses. It was photographed near the new bus station in Chatham on 7 February 2018, awaiting its next working.

Wealden Beeline was another of those small independent companies operating buses in Kent in the 1990s. Services also extended into East Sussex and that is where SSU 780W was heading when photographed in Tunbridge Wells in February 1997. This Duple Dominant-bodied Leyland Leopard bus had come from Scottish operator Grahams of Paisley.

In the 1990s Kent was a really fascinating place for those seeking out independent buses. Yet another business was Kent Coach Tours, who were the proud owner of this forty-eight-seat dual-purpose Leyland National. NFN 85R had been new to East Kent and is seen alongside the former Whitbread Brewery offices in Faversham in the summer of 1995.

Travel Eagle was a short-lived bus operation around the Tonbridge area in the late 1980s and early 1990s. A fleet of second-hand Leyland Nationals was employed and the example here is NWT 702M. This fifty-two-seat bus had started life with West Yorkshire Road Car as fleet number 1414. It is seen crossing over the railway in Tonbridge in mid-1989.

Griffin Bus, associated with North London/Hertfordshire operator Sullivan Buses, also ran services in the vicinity of Tonbridge during the first decade of the twenty-first century. Seen on Mount Pleasant Road in Tunbridge Wells is A634 BCN, a former Northern General MCW Mark II Metrobus. This photograph was taken on 7 July 2009, not long before operations ceased.

The Kings Ferry is a long-established and high-quality coach operation based in Gillingham. It was purchased by National Express in 2007, but has been maintained as a separate business. On 2 April 2007 the company was running the Dockside Shuttle from Chatham railway station, where GN07 FDF was photographed. This Alexander Dennis Enviro200 thirty-eight-seat bus was purchased new earlier in that year. The Dockside Shuttle has since ceased operating.

Sittingbourne operator Chalkwell Coaches can trace its history back to the 1930s, but only entered the stage carriage market in the 1980s. Today it operates a good number of tendered bus routes around the Swale area. Seen in Sheerness-on-Sea in spring 1991 is TKM 108X, an ex-Maidstone Boro'line Bedford YMT/Wadham Stringer saloon.

Prior to the early 1980s, there were very few independent concerns running stage carriage services in Kent. One exception was Drew's of Canterbury, operating a route to St Augustine's Hospital. The regular performer in 1974 was JAR 622G, a Bedford VAM70/Duple (Midland) bus purchased new in 1969. It is seen having a layover between duties in Canterbury bus station. Drew's ceased operating in 1975 and the service passed to East Kent.

Though it has since ceased trading, Coastal Buses built up quite a sizeable network of routes in the early years of the twenty-first century. These were mainly around the Hastings and Rye areas of Sussex, but at least one route ventured into Kent. The company's GU52 HAX is seen passing over the railway line and Tunbridge Wells Central station sometime around 2005. This vehicle, a Dennis Dart with Alexander bodywork (to Plaxton's design), was new to Coastal in 2002.

A company trading under the name of Kingsman tendered for the 666 route between Faversham and Ashford, receiving two dedicated Mercedes O530 forty-two-seat saloons for these duties. One of these, KT04 BUS, named *Pride of Faversham*, is seen outside Ashford International railway station on 11 October 2007. The service has since been given to another operator.

Poynters Coaches, operating out of a yard in Wye near Ashford, gained several subsidised services in rural Kent. An interesting fleet was maintained and, in December 1998, included YRN 814V. This Leyland National 2 had been new as a forty-four-seat bus to Ribble Motor Services. Poynters ceased trading in 2017.

Regent Coaches of Whitstable have been in business since 1970, but have only recently started operating bus services, mainly under Kent County Council contracts. One such service is the 649, a Canterbury local route. In use on such a duty is YX09 FNF, an Alexander Dennis Enviro200 twenty-nine-seat bus, purchased new in May 2009. It was photographed on 4 February 2010 about to enter Canterbury bus station.

Donsway, a Faversham area operator, took over a few rural routes from East Kent in the early 1980s. Operating route 660 is former Maidstone Borough Council HKJ 256N, a Willowbrook-bodied Bedford YRQ seen in Faversham in early 1982. Other interesting buses in the fleet included a former London AEC Swift and, much later, a Leyland National. The company seems to have vanished in the mid-1990s.

Westbus (UK) was formed in 1986 when Australian coach company Westbus PTY took over Swinards of Ashford (Kent) and ADP Travel Services of West London. The company still exists and the Ashford depot has closed. In March 1993 several rural bus routes in Kent were operated, on which two Leyland Nationals are seen in Faversham. The subject of the photograph is KJD 542P, originally numbered LS42 in the London Transport fleet.

Another independent running stage carriage services in Kent in March 1993 was Town & Around. Photographed in Hythe town centre is KBU 892P, a forty-one-seat Leyland National that had been new to Greater Manchester PTE. The company's entry into bus operation did not last very long.

Operating around Maidstone in the early 1990s, Bygone Buses ran a very interesting fleet indeed. One of five prototype Leyland Titans, NHG 732P was photographed in Maidstone's High Street in December 1991. It had originally been a demonstrator for Leyland Vehicles.

Used mainly for private hire and special duties, Bygone Buses owned a former London Transport AEC Routemaster, RM1677 (677 DYE). It is seen at the company's yard in Headcorn on a sunny day in March 1993.

Just arrived in Maidstone High Street in December 1991, Bygone Buses-owned OKE 137P, lettered for coaching duties, is being used on a stage carriage service. By virtue of its 'grant-aid' folding doors it was quite suitable for both roles. This Duple Dominant-bodied Leyland Leopard had been new to Maidstone & District. Ironically, Bygone Buses later sold out to that company.

Kent is famous for growing hops, a variety of which is the Fuggle. The bus company with the same name, Fuggles of Benenden, had been running a few buses services in the area since the 1980s. The network expanded in the 1990s and the vehicles could often be found in the Tunbridge Wells area. In March 1993, GKK 160V was found in the depot yard. As in the previous photograph, this Leyland Leopard coach had been new to Maidstone & District, but carried a Willowbrook forty-nine-seat body. Fuggles have since ceased trading.

Yet another post-deregulation independent to serve Maidstone was Farleigh Coaches. In March 1993, that company's VJG 187J is passing the corner of High Street and Gabriels Hill. This vehicle, an AEC Swift with fifty-one-seat Marshall bodywork, had been new to East Kent in 1970.

Auto-Reps once ran a few bus routes in western Kent. Seen at Chatham in late 1989 is RCN 97N. This Leyland Atlantean AN68/1R with Park Royal bodywork had been new to Tynemouth & District, a Northern General subsidiary. Auto-Reps, not to be confused with Autocar (see page 86), is no longer trading.

Autocar Bus & Coach Services run several rural routes based around the town of Tonbridge. A smart pink and white livery is employed, as seen on G456 MGG, a Duple-bodied Dennis Dart, photographed having a rest in Tunbridge Wells on 18 May 2007. It had been new to Scottish operator Hutchison of Overtown in 1990.

An unusual bus in the Autocar fleet was L298 VRV. This Wadham Stringer-bodied Dennis Dart had been new in 1994 to the London Borough of Redbridge for transporting people with special needs. When photographed on 2 September 2009 it had lost its wheelchair lift and was on normal stage carriage duties on Tonbridge High Street.

For a few years after deregulation Turners of Maidstone ran stage services within the company's home town. Carrying 'Boro'Bus' names, ex-London Country Park Royal-bodied Leyland Atlantean AN68/1R VPB 123M is seen in the centre of Maidstone in March 1993.

Another post-deregulation entrant into stage carriage operation was East Sussex operator Warrens of Ticehurst. Looking very smart in Tunbridge Wells in March 1993 is GKL 827N, a former Maidstone & District Bristol VRT/SL6G with standard ECW bodywork. It was sold later that year to Priory Coaches of Gosport. Warren's operation was later taken over by Hams Travel.

Tentrek, based in South East London, once operated a few bus routes in the Dartford area. It is there, in spring 1988, that we see BDV 316L, which has just arrived with a 494 service. This bus, a Bristol LH6L with unusual dual-purpose bodywork by Marshall, had been new as 1316 in the Western National fleet.

By the spring of 1989 Tentrek had taken on the name of Transcity, once an operator in the Chislehurst area of London. Lettered as 'Transcity Link', this little Bristol LHS6L/ECW, registered OJD 16R, had been new as a twenty-six-seater with London Buses. Once again, the location is Dartford.

Mercury Passenger Services ran a couple of routes in the early 1990s. Seen in Maidstone High Street in January 1992 is D361 JUM. This bus, an Optare CityPacer based on a VW LT55 chassis, had been new to London Buses as OV29 in 1987.

Operated by Mercury Passenger Services on behalf of Kent County Council was K645 SKK, a twenty-seat CVE Omni midibus. In production between 1988 and 1996, this type was never very popular with bus service providers and most were sold to local authorities. K645 SKK was photographed as it had a break between duties in the village of Hoo in March 1993.

Eastonways was a small post-deregulation independent company that ran connecting services to Ramsgate ferry terminal and a few stage carriage routes around the Thanet area. Operating one of the latter in Ramsgate town centre on 4 May 2007 is K990 CBO. New to London Buses in 1993, when it was registered NDZ 3145, it is a Dennis Dart with Wright 'Handybus' bodywork, originally seating twenty-nine passengers.

Another Eastonways bus photographed on 4 May 2007, L227 SWM is seen passing Ramsgate Harbour. This Northern Counties-bodied Dennis Dart had been new to Warrington Borough Transport in 1993. Eastonways went into liquidation in 2013.

One further company running bus services around East Kent was Thanet Bus. One of the more interesting vehicles owned was XNG 773S, an ex-Eastern Counties Leyland National. It was photographed beside Ramsgate Harbour in spring 1991.

One final independent running a bus service into Kent remains to be mentioned. Ensignbus is a large Essex concern that uses the Dartford Crossing to gain access to Bluewater shopping centre and Greenhithe station. That is where 708 (SN11 FFL) was photographed on 6 April 2018. This Alexander Dennis Enviro200 had been new to Wiltshire independent Hatt's Coaches.

A Thanet-based coach company, Kemps was once the owner of this unique AEC Sabre – one of only four manufactured and the only one registered in the UK. This type was the last to be built bearing the AEC name and featured a rear-mounted AEC V8 engine and forty-six-seat ECW coachwork. CBU 636J was delivered new to Best & Sons of London in 1970. By 1981, the date of this photograph, it was found in central Canterbury.

Star Coaches, a Deal private hire and contract operator, were once the proud owners of OEH 22W, seen on relief duties with National Express in Canterbury in November 1986. This Willowbrook-bodied Leyland Leopard coach had been new to Potteries Motor Traction in 1981.

Camden Coaches was a small contract operator based in arches under the main railway line just north of Sevenoaks railway station. At this location in 1976 we see 6330 WJ, a former Sheffield AEC Regent V/Roe H39/30RD new in 1960. Also visible is a former Nottingham double-decker.

The village of Molash lies in an area of outstanding natural beauty some miles north of Ashford. Found there sometime around 1975 was this fine coach, registered 417 FKL, belonging to local operator J. Smith's Coaches. This AEC Reliance with Harrington bodywork had been new in 1959 as CO417 with Maidstone & District.

Buzzlines is a well-known coach company in the Dover area, running regular British and European coach tours for over thirty years. In recent times, the company has gained extra work by operating rail replacement services. On such a duty, at Dover Priory station in July 2005, is T133 AUA. This Plaxton-bodied DAF DE02 double-decker had been new to Capital of West Drayton in London.

Another company to run rail replacement duties on a regular basis is Hams Travel, based at Flimwell in East Sussex, not far from the border in Kent. On 24 October 2009, while the panel in Tonbridge signal box was being renewed, BU57 HAM was awaiting its next spell of work. This forty-five-seat Alexander Dennis Enviro300 had been purchased new by Hams and will shortly depart for Tunbridge Wells and beyond.

Many ferries from Dover to the Continent depart from the Eastern Docks, which are not rail connected. Back in 1981, Townsend Thoresen-liveried MLK 646L, a former London Transport DMS-type Daimler Fleetline/Park Royal, awaits departure at Dover Priory station. It will convey passengers to the ship to the Belgian port of Zeebrugge.

In May 2006 the Dover Priory station to Eastern Docks shuttle was being operated by Optare Excel YJ51 JXG. Seen as it approaches the railhead, it had been new as a demonstrator with the manufacturer.

Scott & Knowles were fruit farmers who operated a small fleet of buses to convey workers to their various locations in the 'Garden of England'. The vehicles were kept in a rural yard near Canterbury and in 1975 that is where these two fine double-deckers were found. On the left is EFN 184, an ex-East Kent 1950 Guy Arab III with 'Utility'-style Park Royal bodywork, while alongside is former Eastbourne Corporation AEC Regent V DHC 654, bodied by East Lancs.

APC were a firm of contractors supplying labourers to the nuclear power station at remote Dungeness. Parked up on the road approach to the long-closed Folkestone East railway station sometime around 1976, AFN 768B was once one of many AEC Regent V buses, bodied by Park Royal, which had been new to East Kent Road Car.